D1432572

DISCARD

Unsolved Mysteries

The Bermuda Triangle

Brian Innes

RAINTREE
STECK-VAUGHN
RSVP PUBLISHERS

A Harcourt Company

Austin · New York
www.steck-vaughn.com

Developed by Brown Partworks
Editor: Lindsey Lowe
Designer: Joan Curtis
Picture Researcher: Brigitte Arora

Raintree Steck-Vaughn Publishers Staff
Project Manager: Joyce Spicer
Editor: Pam Wells

Library of Congress Cataloging-in-Publication Data
Innes, Brian.
  The Bermuda Triangle/by Brian Innes.
    p.   cm.—(Unsolved mysteries)
  Includes bibliographical references and index.
  Summary: Describes disappearances of planes, ships, and people that have
supposedly occurred in the Bermuda Triangle, off the southeast coast of the
United States, and offers possible explanations.
  ISBN 0-8172-5485-4 (Hardcover)
  ISBN 0-8172-5847-7 (Softcover)
    1. Bermuda Triangle—Juvenile literature. [1. Bermuda Triangle.]
  I. Title. II. Series: Innes, Brian. Unsolved mysteries.
  G558.I56   1999
  001.94—dc21   98-28738
                                                     CIP
                                                      AC

Printed and bound in the United States
  3 4 5 6 7 8 9 0 WZ 02 01 00

Acknowledgments

Cover: Peter Poulides/Tony Stone Images; **Page 5:** Douglas Peebles/Corbis; **Page 6:** National Archives/Corbis; **Page 7:** Bermuda Tourism; **Page 9:** Topham Picturepoint; **Page 10:** Magellan Geographix/Corbis; **Page 11:** Fortean Picture Library; **Pages 13, 14, and 17:** Mary Evans Picture Library; **Page 19:** Stephen Frink/Corbis; **Page 21:** NASA/Corbis; **Page 22:** TRH Pictures; **Page 23:** UPI/Corbis; **Page 25:** TRH Pictures; **Page 27:** Guido Alberto Rossi/Image Bank; **Page 28:** TRH Pictures; **Page 29:** Lucas Abreu/Image Bank; **Page 30:** UPI/Corbis-Bettmann; **Page 32:** Pierre Saboulin/PPL; **Page 35:** Historical Picture Archive/Corbis; **Page 37:** The Mariners' Museum/Corbis; **Page 38:** Mary Evans Picture Library; **Pages 39, and 41:** Fortean Picture Library; **Page 43:** Pete Turner/Image Bank; **Page 45:** Archive Photos/Image Bank; **Page 46:** Chris Thomson/Image Bank.

Contents

Mystery of Flight 19

On a clear day in December 1945, a group of planes left Florida. They were never to be seen or heard from again.

This is Florida, photographed from a plane (opposite). Lt. Charles C. Taylor was hoping to see this view at around 4:10 P.M. on December 5, 1945. Instead, he disappeared forever.

At 2:10 P.M. on December 5, 1945, five Avenger torpedo bombers took off from the Naval Air Station at Fort Lauderdale, Florida. They were on a training exercise, listed as Flight 19. The weather was clear, but it was windy. Lieutenant Charles C. Taylor was in command.

SIMPLE EXERCISE

The exercise was a simple one. The planes were to fly almost due east for 56 miles (90 km). When they reached a sandbank called the Hens and Chickens Shoals, they were to use it as a target for bombing practice. Then, they were to fly 67 more miles (108 km) before turning in a northwest direction over the Bahamas. After 73 miles (117 km), they were to turn and fly back to Fort Lauderdale. The time allowed for the exercise was around two hours. Each plane carried a full load of fuel, and all the equipment had been checked. All the planes carried rubber life rafts, and the men had life jackets.

At about 3:45 P.M., a radio call came in from Lt. Taylor. He was heard asking one of the other pilots about the direction they were headed. He was worried about the reading on his compass,

"Both my compasses are out, and I am trying to find Fort Lauderdale, Florida."

LT. CHARLES C. TAYLOR

which should have helped him to find his position. Another instructor, Lt. Robert F. Cox, was in the air near Fort Lauderdale. He called Taylor to see what the problem was. Taylor replied: "Both my compasses are out, and I am trying to find Fort Lauderdale, Florida. I am over land . . . but I don't know how far down, and I don't know how to get to Fort Lauderdale." Then, his voice faded.

Lt. Cox later said this must have meant Flight 19 was heading north, out of his radio range. However, the flight control at Port Everglades thought Taylor was north of Grand Bahama island. At 4:45 P.M., Taylor contacted Port Everglades. He said he would take his flight north, "to make sure we are not over the Gulf of Mexico." He was told to fly due west, but he did not reply.

Five U.S. Navy Avenger bombers in 1942. In 1945 a group like this simply vanished, never to be seen or heard from again.

CONFUSION

During these conversations it was hard for Taylor and flight control to hear each other. Music from Cuban radio stations kept cutting in on the radio signals. At 5:00 P.M., two of the other pilots were heard to say: "If we would just fly west, we would get home." Five minutes later Taylor was heard telling his flight to fly due east instead.

At last, at 5:50 P.M., ground control found Flight 19 on their radar screen. It was about 150 miles (241 km) north of the Bahamas, and 100 miles (161 km) due east of Daytona Beach. By this time night had fallen.

The planes had enough fuel for another hour's flying. But during that hour the planes disappeared forever.

Search planes took off. At 7:30 P.M., a Martin Mariner from Banana River Naval Air Station joined the search. Twenty minutes later, the captain of a ship reported that he had seen the plane catch fire and explode. At the same moment, the tracking signal vanished from the radar screen of the U.S. Coast Guard in Miami. No wreckage from the Mariner, or from the five Avengers, was ever found.

WHAT HAPPENED?

It seems that when Flight 19 was over the Bahamas, Lt. Taylor thought it was over Florida. By leading his flight to the northeast, he had gone even farther from land. As for the Martin Mariner, planes of this type were known as "flying gas tanks." Fumes from the fuel were often present inside the plane. They could have caused an explosion. Those are the known facts.

For several years nobody thought there was anything unusual about what had happened. Then, in the 1950s, unidentified flying objects, or UFOs, became news. Some writers said that UFOs had something to do with the planes that had disappeared. In 1964 Vincent Gaddis wrote an article for the UFO magazine *Flying Saucer Review*. Gaddis titled the article "The Deadly Bermuda Triangle."

The islands of Bermuda. Vincent Gaddis was the first to write about the "Bermuda Triangle."

Bermuda Triangle

In the 1950s and 1960s, people began to count the ships and planes lost in the Atlantic Ocean.

Vincent Gaddis wrote his first article about the Bermuda Triangle in 1964. He wrote an entire book about it in 1965. In this book, called *Invisible Horizons*, he described the Bermuda Triangle as being "the Triangle of Death."

Gaddis noted that a number of ships and planes had mysteriously vanished in the Atlantic Ocean, just off the southeast coast of the United States. Ships had also been found drifting there without their crews. The area lies inside an imaginary line drawn from Miami down to Puerto Rico, then up to the island of Bermuda, and back to Miami. It made a neat triangle.

SEA OF MYSTERY

In his book Gaddis wrote: "This . . . limited area is the scene of disappearances that total far beyond the laws of chance. Despite swift wings and the voice of radio, we still have a world large enough for men and their machines, and ships, to disappear without a trace."

Seamen's tales of the strangeness of the ocean near the islands of Bermuda go back to the time of Christopher Columbus. In 1492, Columbus set sail westward from Spain. He expected to

This map illustration (opposite) shows some of the ships and planes said to have been lost in the "Bermuda Triangle."

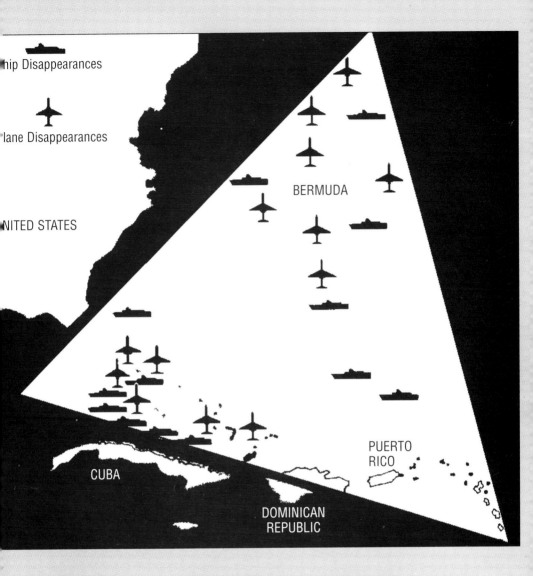

"This . . . limited area is the scene of disappearances that total far beyond the laws of chance."

VINCENT GADDIS

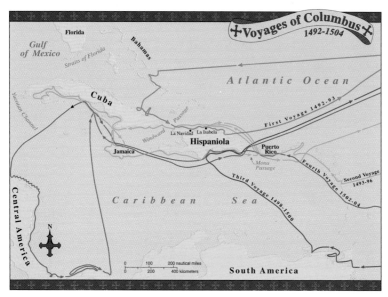

This map gives an idea of the routes Columbus took. The Sargasso Sea lies just to the north of "Hispaniola," which is now Haiti and the Dominican Republic.

keep sailing until he reached China. Instead he discovered the islands of the West Indies. On the way Columbus's ships sailed through the Sargasso Sea. This is a huge area of the Atlantic Ocean. There is often no wind, and sailing ships can drift there for weeks at a time. There is also a great amount of floating seaweed. In fact, the name Sargasso comes from the Portuguese word for seaweed—*sargaço*.

STRANGE HAPPENINGS

Columbus had noticed that while he was in the Sargasso Sea, his compass did not point toward the North Star any more. It pointed more to the west. This is now known as magnetic variation. A compass does not point to the North Pole. It points to the Earth's magnetic north, which is presently near Ellef Ringnes Island, in the upper islands of the Northwest Territories of Canada. But the sailors did not know this at the time. They were very frightened. Later Columbus made a report of his journey. He said that one night a ball of flame fell into the sea. Another night the sailors saw a light flickering in the distance. They thought they had sighted land. But in the morning they found they were nowhere near land.

For hundreds of years after this, sailors told stories of what might happen to ships sailing to or from the Americas. Some of the stories were true. During the 16th and 17th centuries, for example, many Spanish sailing ships were lost in hurricanes. Some were captured by pirates. Many sank. But nobody thought there was anything particularly odd about the triangle of sea lying between Bermuda and the Florida coast.

This is the book that Vincent Gaddis wrote in 1965. In it, he suggested that strange things were happening in the Bermuda Triangle and other parts of the Atlantic.

MORE THAN CHANCE

Then, in September 1950, a journalist named E. V. W. Jones made a list of unexplained disappearances in the area. It was printed by one newspaper on September 16, and appeared in other Florida newspapers on the next day. People's interest in the mysteries of the Bermuda Triangle had begun.

Writers on the subject, including Vincent Gaddis, claim that more than 150 ships and planes have vanished in the Triangle during the past 150 years. For more than a century, one of the great mysteries of the sea has been what happened to the ship *Mary Celeste*. It is a story that is often told in books on the Bermuda Triangle.

The *Mary Celeste*

One of the most famous mysteries of all is that of the ship Mary Celeste. But was this linked to the Bermuda Triangle?

This is a picture of the Mary Celeste *drifting at sea (opposite). It first appeared in* A Great Sea Mystery—*a book about the ship's disappearance.*

The *Mary Celeste* was a 280-ton sailing ship. It was found drifting, with nobody on board, by a ship named *Dei Gratia* on December 4, 1872. Both ships had been loading cargo in New York in early November. Captain Briggs, of the *Mary Celeste*, sailed for Genoa, in Italy, on November 7. His wife and daughter, as well as a crew of eight men, were also aboard. Captain Moorhouse, of the other ship, the *Dei Gratia*, sailed for Gibraltar on November 15.

Three weeks later, Moorhouse sighted the *Mary Celeste*. The sails were up, but the ship was moving strangely through the water. As the *Dei Gratia* caught up with it, Moorhouse sent some men in a small boat to have a closer look.

A GHOST SHIP

There were several stories of what they found. Some people said that a meal was still cooking on the stove. The captain's belongings were still aboard, and his daughter's toys lay on his bed. The cargo was said to be untouched, making it unlikely that the ship had been attacked by thieves or pirates. There was also a full supply of food and water.

The sails were up, but the ship was moving strangely through the water.

This drawing shows what crew members from Dei Gratia *found aboard the* Mary Celeste.

However, the ship's papers, except for the daily log, had gone. So had the navigation instruments. The last entry in the log was for November 24—10 days before the *Dei Gratia* arrived on the scene. At that time the *Mary Celeste* had been only about 100 miles (161 km) west of the mid-Atlantic Ridge— a long way from the Bermuda Triangle.

Moorhouse's men sailed the *Mary Celeste* to Gibraltar. But what had happened to Captain Briggs, his wife and daughter, and his crew? There were all kinds of stories.

WAS MOORHOUSE INVOLVED?

Some people said Moorhouse and his crew were pirates. It was claimed that they had killed everybody on the *Mary Celeste*. Another story suggested that Moorhouse had planted some of his own men among the crew of the *Mary Celeste* while both ships had been in New York. Then, in the middle of the ocean, they had taken over the ship and thrown everybody else overboard.

The only known facts about this strange story are that 11 people vanished from the ship and were never seen again. Also, the *Mary Celeste* was not damaged, although a few sails were slightly torn. The ship was sailing without anybody to steer and had probably done so for 10 days before being found.

MILES FROM BERMUDA

There is one other important fact, however. The mystery of *Mary Celeste* cannot have happened in the Bermuda Triangle, as has been suggested by many people. When the ship was found drifting, it was between the Azores and Portugal. This is more than 3,000 miles (4,827 km) east of Bermuda.

And, finally, there is one piece of fiction. The *Mary Celeste* is often wrongly called the *Marie Celeste*. In January 1884, some 11 years after the *Dei Gratia* found the abandoned ship, a young writer named Arthur Conan Doyle had published a short story. He was later to create the famous detective Sherlock Holmes, but this Conan Doyle story was about a ship called the *Marie Celeste*. Because the story was so much like the real mystery, many people thought it was true. That was how the mix-up over the name began.

The mystery of Mary Celeste cannot have happened in the Bermuda Triangle. . . .

TALES FROM THE TRIANGLE

So did the story of *Mary Celeste* have anything to do with the Bermuda Triangle? The answer is, probably not. There are, however, other mysterious stories of disappearances—of ships or crews—that certainly did happen in the waters of the Bermuda Triangle.

Vanishing Ships

Between 1866 and 1945, many ships were lost in the Bermuda Triangle. These are just some of their stories.

In 1866 the Swedish ship *Lotta* disappeared somewhere north of the island of Haiti in the West Indies. This was within the area that later came to be known as the Bermuda Triangle. Two years later, the Spanish ship *Viego* vanished in the same area. In 1880, the British sail-training ship *Atalanta* was lost. There were more than 290 young cadets aboard. In 1884 it was the Italian ship *Miramon*'s turn to disappear.

20TH-CENTURY MYSTERIES

By the turn of the 20th century, Joshua Slocum had become the world's most famous sailor. Between 1895 and 1898, he had sailed alone around the world in his yacht, *Spray*.

On November 14, 1909, Slocum set out from Martha's Vineyard, in Massachusetts. Nobody knew where he was headed. Somewhere to the south, he and his boat disappeared. Perhaps it was in the Bermuda Triangle. However, the American writer Edward Rowe Stowe said that Slocum had been run down by a steamship, somewhere south of the Virgin Islands in the Caribbean Sea. This would have placed the ship about 1,000 miles (1,609 km) from Bermuda.

This painting shows Joshua Slocum sailing alone around the world aboard his yacht, Spray (opposite). In 1909, Slocum and his boat disappeared.

16

By the beginning of the 20th century, Joshua Slocum had become the world's most famous sailor.

In March 1918, there was a more mysterious disappearance. The USS *Cyclops* was one of the largest ships in the U.S. Navy at that time. On March 4, *Cyclops* sailed from Barbados, headed for Norfolk, Virginia. It never arrived. Although the ship carried a radio, no call for help was ever received. A month later the Navy had to accept that the *Cyclops*, along with 293 men, was lost. At that time the U.S. was at war with Germany. It was possible that the ship had been sunk by a German submarine or a battleship.

STORMY WEATHER

A huge search began for the missing ship, but nothing was found. Years later a senior Navy officer said he thought *Cyclops* had sunk during a hurricane, although there were no published reports of severe storms in the area at the time. However, 60 years later writer Larry Kusche looked at the weather center records in Asheville, North Carolina. On March 9, 1918, gale warnings had been issued from Maine to North Carolina. On March 10, winds had reached 60 miles per hour (mph) (96.5 kilometers per hour [kmph]) at Norfolk. Then, in 1968, Navy diver Dean Hawes found a wreck in deep water off Norfolk. He said it looked like *Cyclops*.

CAPTURED BY SMUGGLERS?

In the 1920s, several American ships were suddenly lost in the Bermuda Triangle. This was during the time when there was trade with Cuba that was against the law. Navy officials suggested that perhaps these ships had been captured by smugglers. Whatever the truth, nothing more was discovered about what had finally happened to them.

Two divers look at a sunken ship off the Virgin Islands. Could it be that other lost ships lie, still undiscovered, beneath the waters of the Bermuda Triangle?

OTHER DISAPPEARANCES

Many other ships and their crews have vanished in the Bermuda Triangle. People have claimed that this is due to a mysterious power. However, it could just be that the area is subject to particularly rough storms. Proof of this is the fact that the crews of many ships thought to be missing were later rescued. They have told stories of how they were forced to leave their ships after they had been damaged by bad weather.

The crew of the fishing boat *John and Mary* was rescued off Cape May, New Jersey, on March 8, 1932. Five weeks later the wreck was found, still afloat, south of Bermuda. On August 27, 1935, the Italian liner *Rex* rescued five men from a yacht, *La Dahama*. On September 1, the wreck of *La Dahama* was seen drifting 700 miles (1,126 km) northeast of Bermuda.

These are some of the stories, from 1866 to the outbreak of World War II in 1939, that have appeared in books on the Bermuda Triangle. After the mystery of Flight 19 in 1945, interest turned to the skies.

Vanishing Planes

The planes
on Flight
19 were
not the
only ones
to be lost
over the
Bermuda
Triangle.

On January 27, 1948, a British airliner named *Star Tiger* left London for Bermuda. It was a type known as a Tudor IV. The crew was very experienced and had flown to Bermuda before.

On the first leg of the flight, *Star Tiger* landed at Lisbon, Portugal. It stopped there overnight so that some minor repairs could be done. In particular, one of the compasses was not working. Next morning the plane was flown to the Azores, where the captain was given a weather report. There were going to be strong winds over the Atlantic, so the captain decided to wait. The compass was still not working properly.

STRONG WINDS BLOWING

There was also another British plane waiting in the Azores. It was a Lancastrian. It, too, was headed for Bermuda. On January 29, the Lancastrian took off. It was followed an hour later, at 3:34 P.M., by *Star Tiger*.

The expected flight time was 12 hours and 30 minutes. However, the winds were stronger than forecast, and the Lancastrian did not land in Bermuda until 4:11 A.M. Because of the wind, *Star Tiger*'s captain radioed that his expected

A photograph
of Earth (opposite)
taken from space.
It shows storm
clouds over the
Atlantic Ocean.
Some people say
that such storms
are behind many of
the disappearances
in the Bermuda
Triangle.

20

There were going to be strong winds over the Atlantic, so the captain decided to wait.

This is an airliner of the Star Tiger Tudor IV type. The planes regularly flew the London-to-Bermuda route. Star Tiger vanished in 1948.

arrival time should be changed to 5:00 A.M. The last signal from *Star Tiger* was at 3:15 A.M. Bermuda got a fix on its position. At 3:50 A.M. the Bermuda operator radioed the plane. There was no reply. Fifteen minutes later there was still no reply. At 4:40 A.M. he reported a "state of emergency"—meaning that the emergency services were called out.

At 7:15 A.M. (3:15 A.M. local Bermuda time), a U.S. Army Air Force search plane took off from Bermuda. During that day, 25 other planes joined the search. After five days nothing had been found. It seemed that soon after 3:15 A.M., *Star Tiger* had just vanished from the sky.

COMPLETE MYSTERY

Star Tiger carried a full load of fuel, enough for a flight lasting nearly 16 hours. Although one of the compasses was faulty, there were two others aboard the plane that should have been working normally. At the plane's last known position, the weather was calm. There were no electrical storms. Strangest of all, there had been no radio call for help.

22

The British Ministry of Civil Aviation held an official investigation. It reported that, even if the plane's radio had failed, it should have been able to find its own way to Bermuda without much problem. The report decided that, "no more baffling [puzzling] problem has ever been presented for investigation."

STAR ARIEL

A year later a sister plane of *Star Tiger*, the *Star Ariel*, vanished just as mysteriously. On a clear morning, January 17, 1949, the plane took off from Bermuda, bound for Kingston, Jamaica. The last radio message was received in Bermuda an hour later. Four hours later Kingston called Bermuda. *Star Ariel* was due in 15 minutes, and nothing had been heard from the plane. In the late afternoon other aircraft went out to search for it. No wreckage was ever found.

There had been another disappearance three weeks earlier. An old Douglas DC-3 was booked to carry 27 passengers from Puerto Rico to Miami. In the late evening of December 27, 1948, it took off from the airport at San Juan.

Just before dawn the copilot reported the plane's position as 50 miles (80 km) south of Miami. After that there was no more contact.

The plane carried enough fuel to fly for seven and a half hours. Ten and a half hours after it had left Puerto Rico, on the morning

Passengers leave San Juan for Miami in 1950. Two years earlier a similar flight had ended in mystery.

23

of December 28, the Coast Guard ordered a search for the plane. Nothing was found. Later it was decided that the copilot must have been mistaken about the plane's last reported position. During the flight the wind had shifted from northwest to northeast. Without radar, and without a radio that worked, the DC-3 could have drifted 50 miles (80 km) farther to the west. It probably went down in the Gulf of Mexico, but nobody had searched in that area.

Some time after it took off, a cargo ship reported "a plane in flames overhead."

CREATING A MYTH

Following these disappearances, other planes were also said to have been lost in the Bermuda Triangle, or "just to the north." However, some of the disappearances actually happened farther north than "just to the north" of the triangle drawn between Miami, Puerto Rico, Bermuda, and back to Miami.

For example, a U.S. Air Force plane crashed into the ocean in 1951. It was some 500 miles (800 km) southwest of the coast of Ireland—over 2,000 miles (3,200 km) from Bermuda. A British troop air transport, flying from the Azores to Newfoundland, radioed a call for help in 1953. At that time it was some 360 miles (580 km) from Newfoundland—nearly 1,500 miles (2,400 km) from Bermuda.

However, on November 9, 1956, a Navy Martin Marlin was lost closer to the triangle. Some time after it took off, a cargo ship reported "a plane in flames

This photograph was taken from a U.S. Navy helicopter in 1950. It shows an early version of the Martin Marlin "flying boat." It is the same type as the plane lost in November 1956.

overhead." Twenty minutes later the ship radioed that an explosion had been heard. The disaster took place about 400 miles (644 km) southeast of New York, and the same distance from Bermuda. The loss of this Martin Marlin was very similar to the loss of the Martin Mariner that had gone out on the search for Flight 19—11 years before.

FURTHER STORIES

To include these stories, and others, in their books, writers on the Bermuda Triangle have had to widen the area they cover. Often they included most of the northwest Atlantic and part of the Gulf of Mexico. But in the course of their investigations, they have also found more missing ships to add to the mystery.

More Sea Losses

Many ships were lost at sea in World War II. But after the war ended, there were others that were missing for no reason.

The USS *Cyclops* had vanished off Norfolk, Virginia, in March 1918. Over 23 years later, two of her sister ships, *Proteus* and *Nereus*, also disappeared. Once owned by the U.S. Navy, both ships had been sold to a Canadian company in 1940. They were used to carry bauxite back from the West Indies to Norfolk. Bauxite is an aluminium ore. It was of great importance to the U.S. military aircraft industry, which was rapidly increasing in size at the time. This was due to the war against Germany that was being fought throughout Europe.

WAR VICTIM?

Proteus left St. Thomas, in the Virgin Islands, on November 23, 1941. It was headed for Norfolk, Virginia, right through the Bermuda Triangle. But it never arrived. This was just two weeks before the Japanese attacked the American military bases at Pearl Harbor, Hawaii. This attack brought the U.S. into World War II.

Although the U.S. was not officially at war with Germany until December 11, the country was already sending military supplies to Britain, which had been at war with Germany since 1939. After the war had ended in 1945, secret

This is the port of St. Thomas in the Virgin Islands (opposite). To reach it from the U.S., ships have to cross the waters of the Bermuda Triangle.

26

It was headed for Norfolk . . . through the Bermuda Triangle. But it never arrived.

German records showed *Proteus* had probably been sunk on November 25, 1941 by a U-boat, or a German submarine.

On December 10, 1941, *Nereus* had left St. Thomas for Norfolk. It, too, disappeared in the Bermuda Triangle. The Navy thought it likely that *Nereus* had also been "torpedoed and sunk by a German U-boat."

This is the view along the deck of a U-boat as it dives. German U-boats sank many ships during World War II.

TRIANGLE TRAGEDIES

On October 22, 1944, a Navy airship reported that it had seen the wreckage of a ship just off the coast of Florida. It was the *Rubicon*, a large Cuban cargo ship. Coast Guards from Miami boarded the ship. They found that the lifeboats were missing, but the crew's belongings—and a dog—were still aboard.

The mooring cable, which is used to tie a ship to a harbor wall, was broken and hanging over the side. The final entry in the ship's log was dated September 26, when the ship was in Havana, Cuba. The Coast Guard said the *Rubicon* must have broken free from its moorings when a huge hurricane struck Havana. It had been drifting northward for weeks. However, the crew was never found.

On March 6, 1948, the Miami weather bureau reported very heavy winds. The next day, the winds from the northeast continued to blow at a speed of 48 miles per hour (77 kmph). The following day the search was on for a 16-foot (4.8-m) dinghy from the yacht *Evelyn K*. Al Snider, America's most famous jockey at the time, had gone out on a fishing trip with two friends. They had left the yacht anchored and were now missing.

For several days 30 planes searched the waters south of Florida. A reward of $15,000 was offered. Some time later the dinghy was found in the swamps of Ten Thousand Islands, near Everglades City. It was empty. No trace of the men was ever found.

OTHER STRANGE LOSSES

On April 5, 1950, the Costa Rican freighter *Sandra* sailed from Savannah, Georgia. It was headed for Venezuela, in South America, and was equipped with a radio. The journey should have taken nine days.

Cuba is often subjected to high winds and hurricanes. This is Havana after a storm. The waves are still high. Was the Rubicon *a victim of such stormy seas?*

The Bermuda Triangle lies in what is known as "the hurricane belt." This is Miami Beach, Florida, at the start of Hurricane Donna on September 9, 1960.

The ship had still not arrived in Venezuela by April 19. There was no report of any call for help. The Coast Guard gave up searching for the ship on May 29.

DOUBLE TROUBLE

The *Southern Isles* and the *Southern Districts* were two former Navy ships that had been used for carrying tanks around the world. They were changed to carry sulfur from Louisiana to Maine. On October 5, 1951, *Southern Isles* sank off Cape Hatteras, North Carolina.

Men on board other nearby ships were astonished. The lights on *Southern Isles* suddenly disappeared. A few minutes later, when they reached the scene, the ship had vanished. Six surviving crew members were rescued from the water. They said it seemed that the ship had suddenly broken in half. It went down so quickly that there had been no chance of sending a radio message for help.

Three years later, in December 1954, the *Southern Districts* was also lost. The last radio message, on December 5, reported that it was just off the South Carolina coast. On December 7, a Navy ship named the *Anacostia* sighted *Southern Districts* off Charleston, "battling high seas and gale winds." The ship was never seen again. Only a life ring with the name *Southern Districts* on it was found. This was picked up off the Florida coast on January 2, 1955.

. . . the Anacostia *sighted* Southern Districts *. . . "battling high seas and gale winds."*

The Coast Guard were very concerned by these two disappearances. They immediately canceled the official trading certificates of all ships of this type so that they could no longer carry on business legally. A full investigation was held on January 3. A sailor told how he had left the *Southern Districts* a week before it had sailed. He said it was because *Southern Districts* was "just one big bucket of rust."

ANOTHER *MARY CELESTE*?

One of the strangest stories to take place in the area of the Bermuda Triangle concerns the trimaran yacht *Teignmouth Electron*. A trimaran is a sailboat with three hulls that sit in the water, and a central mast. The hulls, positioned side-by-side, are held together by strips of metal. The *Teignmouth Electron* was one of the sail-boats entered in a race around the world. Its captain was an Englishman named Donald Crowhurst. In his last radio message, Crowhurst had suggested that he was going to win the race.

MAN OVERBOARD?

On July 10, 1969, *Teignmouth Electron* was found drifting in the mid-Atlantic. It was 700 miles (1,126 km) from the Azores. There was no sign of Crowhurst. The ship's log, other papers, and equipment were still aboard. There was no sign of damage to the boat. At first, it was thought that Crowhurst had been washed overboard. Then, it was discovered that Crowhurst had not sailed around the world at all, as he had claimed. In fact, he had spent 243 days cruising in the

In 1969, Donald Crowhurst set off in his yacht to race around the world. He never returned. His yacht was a trimaran, similar to the one shown here.

southern Atlantic, making false radio reports of his position. It seemed that, in the end, he had realized that his trick would be discovered. Although nobody will ever know the truth, it is possible that he jumped overboard rather than be found out.

A HAPPY ENDING

The story of Bill Verity is equally odd, but in a different way. Many writers on the Bermuda Triangle claim that he and his boat, *Brendan the Bold*, vanished in August 1969. Verity was an experienced sailor and had sailed from Ireland, headed for Florida.

On August 21 the Coast Guard asked all ships to be on the lookout for Verity. They were becoming worried because his ship was thought to be near the path of Hurricane Debbie. Nobody had seen or heard from Verity and his ship for days. However, Verity and *Brendan the Bold* suddenly turned up safely at San Salvador Island, in the Bahamas, on September 14. Verity described his experiences in the hurricane and said that at one time he thought he was "a goner." He had certainly not vanished.

MODERN MYTHS

These stories are just some of the 150 unexplained disappearances that are said to have happened in the Bermuda Triangle. In some cases, however, the disappearances were hundreds of miles away from the Triangle, on the other side of the Atlantic. In others, ships and planes have been lost during storms. And, in some cases, there has been no disappearance at all.

The question therefore remains: Is there any truth in the mysterious powers of the Bermuda Triangle, or is it just a 20th-century myth?

Other Triangles

Many ships have been lost in the waters off Japan. This print by Hokusai (opposite) shows a boat struggling through a great wave.

Vincent Gaddis first came up with the name Bermuda Triangle in 1964. Later he wrote: "Over all the seas of the Earth, there is only one other . . . area where mysterious disappearances have repeatedly occurred. This is the . . . 'Devil's Sea' region in the Pacific, south of Japan, and east of the Bonin Islands. Here, too, in a limited area, the usual dangers that menace [threaten] planes and ships fail to explain why it is seldom that wreckage or bodies are found."

THE "DEVIL'S SEA"

The story of the "Devil's Sea" begins with the loss of the Japanese ship *Daigo Kaiyo Maru* on September 26, 1952. Two weeks before, there had been a huge earthquake under the sea. It had been caused by the explosion of an underwater volcano. This was near the Myojin-sho Reefs, about 200 miles (322 km) south of Tokyo. Smaller explosions continued for many days. The *Daigo Kaiyo Maru* was sent to the area. The ship carried a crew of 22, and nine scientists. They wanted to study the seabed.

The following day, the Japanese Coast Guard reported that the ship had disappeared. An expert said it must have been sucked into the

"It is highly probable that a tidal wave washed the vessel to the bottom."

DIRECTOR OF THE MARITIME (SEA) SAFETY BOARD

hole left in the seabed after the volcano had exploded. The director of the Maritime, or sea, Safety Board said: "It is highly probable that a tidal wave washed the vessel to the bottom." Tidal waves are enormous waves that often follow volcanic activity.

DANGEROUS REEFS

Planes and ships searched the area. They found some pieces of the ship. A patrol boat picked up a floating marker buoy. Ships carry buoys so that they can put them into the water to warn other ships of dangers such as rocks. The buoy found by the search teams had the name *Daigo Kaiyo Maru* on it. Following this, a warning was issued to all ships. They were told to keep clear of the Myojin-sho Reefs.

. . . nine other fishing boats had disappeared in the same area in the past five years.

On September 30, *The New York Times* reported that "a second Japanese vessel may have been swallowed up by the volcanic explosion and tidal wave." This was the *No. 2 Tosui Maru*. In fact, the ship's engine had failed. It was saved the same day. The ship had no radio, so it had been unable to call for help.

RISING NUMBERS

On January 4, 1955, another Japanese ship, *Shihyo Maru*, was also given up for lost. The ship was not answering radio calls. On January 14, Japanese newspapers reported that nine other fishing boats had

This photograph was taken in the 1930s. It shows Japanese fishing boats unloading their catch of sardines. These boats would not have carried radios.

disappeared in the same area in the past five years. They had all been lost about 30 miles (48 km) southeast of Mikura Island. This island is about 150 miles (240 km) south of Tokyo.

The newspapers said these boats had disappeared "because of wind, rough seas, or engine trouble." As if to prove the papers right, the *Shihyo Maru* reached port the next day. The crew said that their radio had failed. That was why they could not be contacted.

OUT OF CONTACT

At that time very few Japanese fishing boats carried radios. When they were in trouble, they could not call for help. If they sank, they simply vanished.

The weather in waters fished by the Japanese is often bad. Somewhere between 400 and 500 losses at sea were reported each year before these boats had radios. Nevertheless, in the 1950s stories began to spread in Japan that ships were vanishing "because of some unknown power connected with the Atomic Age." It had only been about 10 years since the atomic bomb attacks on the cities of Hiroshima and Nagasaki toward the end of World War II. The Japanese were still afraid of atomic power.

NEW DANGER AREA

Then a newspaperman gave a name to the area south of Mikura Island. He may have meant "magic sea" or "ghost sea." However, when someone put the characters of the Japanese alphabet into English, the words came out as meaning "devil sea"—and the name stuck. Some people decided that the "Devil's Sea" was the same shape as the Bermuda Triangle.

However, nobody agrees on where the triangle is. Some draw an imaginary line southeast from Tokyo to Guam, passing Iwo Jima. Then the line goes east to Wake Island, and back to Tokyo. Others say that this line goes southeast from Tokyo to Guam, then west from Guam to the Philippine Islands, and northeast to Tokyo.

This magazine cover from 1930 suggests that ships in the Atlantic Ocean were trapped by a mysterious force under the sea.

WORLD OF TRIANGLES

Ivan T. Sanderson was the science editor of *Argosy* magazine. He was interested by the Devil's Sea and the Bermuda Triangle. He decided to check the reports of ships

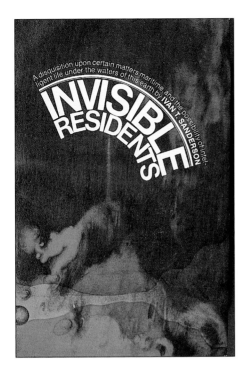

The cover of Ivan T. Sanderson's book. In it, he offered explanations for many sea mysteries.

and planes that had been lost in other parts of the world. He was sure there must be more than two areas where ships and planes vanish mysteriously.

The result of Sanderson's research was his idea of "Vile Vortices." A vortex is like a whirlpool, where liquid moves fast in a circular motion. Then everything around it is drawn into its center. Vortices are two or more of these whirlpools. Sanderson's Vile Vortices were areas all over the globe where mysterious disappearances have happened. He also claimed that they were areas where UFOs, or unidentified flying objects, had been sighted! Sanderson claimed that if you drew straight lines to join all these areas together you would have a series of equal-sided triangles.

NO SCIENTIFIC PROOF

Sanderson's idea makes an interesting pattern on a globe. However, there is little proof of mysterious disappearances in most of these triangles. Two are on land, one is in the northwest corner of Africa, the other is in the mountains of Afghanistan. This, however, did not stop Sanderson from writing in his book *Invisible Residents*: "Planes, ships and subs [submarines] have been disappearing all over the world. But it has to be admitted that many more are reported to have done so in these areas than in any others."

What Is the Truth?

Can there really be a mysterious power in the waters of the Bermuda Triangle? Some think it is pure fiction.

It seems that almost every so-called mysterious disappearance in the Bermuda Triangle can be explained. In many cases books that have been written about the Triangle actually have some of their facts wrong. As for the "Devil's Sea" and the "Vile Vortices"—they appear to be entirely imaginary. Most writers, however, still believe otherwise. Charles Berlitz is the author of many books on the subject, including *The Bermuda Triangle* and *Without a Trace*. He wrote: "Large and small boats have disappeared without leaving wreckage, as if they and their crews have been snatched into another dimension [another time and place]."

LINKS WITH ATLANTIS

Legend has it that a great city named Atlantis sank beneath the sea thousands of years ago. Charles Berlitz believed that the ruins of Atlantis could be found under the sea off the small island of North Bimini, in the Bahamas. He wondered if anything remained of that ancient civilization.

Film producer Alan Landsburg took this idea a step further. He suggested there was a "space corridor" for UFOs running across the Atlantic

The mystery of the Bermuda Triangle may never be solved. However, many people have written books about the subject (opposite).

40

In many cases books that have been written about the Triangle actually have some of their facts wrong.

Ocean. Spaceships could use this to land on Earth. He also suggested that something had sucked the missing ships down so quickly "that nothing was left behind for searchers to see." Perhaps, he said, there had been a group of visitors from space living on the Bahama plateau before it sank beneath the sea. They might have been highly advanced in science and math. They would have had an energy source to heat and light their homes and power their spaceships.

POWERFUL ENERGY
What if, said Landsburg, the men from space had accidentally dropped the power supply in deep water somewhere within the Bermuda Triangle? Landsburg suggested that any ships or planes entering the area would be affected by it.

This ties in with a theory put forward in 1933. An American named Edgar Cayce had suggested that the advanced scientific knowledge of the ancient people of Atlantis had been based on the "Terrible Crystals." He said these crystals, which are clumps of colorless, transparent minerals, were used to draw power from the stars. He also claimed that unused energy ran off into the ground. It built up to dangerous levels and in the end had caused Atlantis to blow up. Could this also be behind the mysterious disappearances in the Bermuda Triangle?

UP IN THE CLOUDS
Landsburg's suggestion of a mysterious power source was followed by a number of strange stories. On December 4, 1970, Bruce Gernon, Jr., took off to fly from the Andros Islands, in the Bahamas, to Palm Beach, Florida. Just after takeoff Gernon approached

42

These wispy clouds are called cirrus clouds. They consist of tiny ice crystals. Perhaps Bruce Gernon, Jr., had mistaken one for something more mysterious?

a "strange, cigar-shaped cloud." He climbed rapidly to avoid it, but it seemed to surround the plane.

Gernon said he saw a small open tunnel in the cloud. The walls of the tunnel were glowing white and small clouds were floating about inside. Gernon tried to dive through the tunnel into the blue sky ahead. He noted that the plane suddenly seemed to move very fast. When they came out of the tunnel, the compass was spinning around.

LOST TIME

Spotting land ahead, Gernon decided that it must be the Bimini islands, north of the Bahamas. Then he saw it was Miami Beach. When he landed at Palm Beach he looked at his watch. He had made the flight in only 45 minutes. The same route normally took 75 minutes. He had also used much less fuel than usual.

Lt. Charles Taylor, the leader of Flight 19—which disappeared in the Bermuda Triangle in 1945—had also reported compass failure. As a result, it has been suggested that the Bermuda Triangle is a place where all sorts of unusual magnetic energy occurs. Magnetic energy is a natural force that draws objects toward a particular thing or place.

. . . there is no . . . reason why so many ships and planes are lost in the area.

PROJECT MAGNET

In 1963 a magazine named *UFO Investigator* claimed that it had discovered a secret Navy project. It had the code name "Project Magnet." The magazine said it was linked to an investigation into UFOs.

The project used Super Constellation aircraft fitted with special equipment. According to the magazine, the planes had discovered "peculiar magnetic forces" when they flew over the sea near Florida. The report claimed that the Navy was investigating how UFOs were controlled and powered.

MAPPING THE WORLD

Following this report, a leaflet about Project Magnet was made available to the public. The Navy claimed that the purpose of the project was simply to make new maps of all the oceans of the world.

They said it was important that different areas of magnetic energy be clearly marked on maps. Many of the maps still used on ships and planes were over 30 years old. The Navy claimed that they were trying to bring them up to date. At the same time, they denied that anything unusual had been found over, or near, the Bermuda Triangle.

Nevertheless, writers on the Triangle continue to claim that there is no logical reason why so many ships and planes are lost in the area. But is this true? On average some 150,000 ships cross the Triangle every year. The Coast Guard has reported that as many as 10,000 may radio for help (nearly always in bad weather), and some 100 losses are recorded every year. That is a very small proportion.

NATURAL FORCES

Hurricanes often happen in the West Indies and the Gulf of Mexico. These high winds move at speeds of more than 75 mph (121 kmph). From June through October the average number is seven each year. They travel northward, up through the Bermuda Triangle,

This is a Super Constellation aircraft. In the 1960s the U.S. Navy used this type of plane to search the waters of the Bermuda Triangle.

A hurricane battering small yachts and other ships in the harbor of Saint Martin. This is an island in the West Indies, where hurricanes happen every year.

causing terrible damage to Florida and many other areas farther up the east coast of the United States. There are other fierce storms, too. Sailors have feared the gales and high seas in the area for centuries.

NO MYSTERY?

Of the many ships lost each year, most are fishing boats and small pleasure craft. They are easily broken up by pounding waves. When a search is made, the area that has to be covered may be more than 10,000 square miles (25,900 square km). It is easy to miss tiny pieces of wreckage. Many of the larger ships that have disappeared were old, badly loaded, or carrying too much. They would easily sink in a bad storm.

Many things point to the fact that the Bermuda Triangle may be more dangerous than other parts of the ocean. But this might be because of sudden storms or because people sailing for pleasure may not be experienced. There seems to be no proof, but many people really believe this is a mysterious "Triangle of Death."

Glossary

atomic bomb A bomb that uses the power of nuclear energy. Nuclear energy is the powerful force produced when the nucleus, or central part, of an atom is split or joined to another atom.

cadets Students at a military, naval, or police training school.

cargo The goods carried by a ship, plane, or other vehicle.

civilization The level of growth in language, science, and arts of a particular people. The Aztec civilization is an example.

dinghy A small, open boat driven by oars or sails. Often carried on larger boats in case of emergency.

fumes Strong-smelling air caused by smoke, gas, or chemicals.

gale A very strong wind.

investigation A thorough examination of a person or thing.

logical reason Something that makes sense according to known scientific reasoning.

magnetic variation A compass points toward Earth's magnetic north, which is slightly east or west of the North Pole. This is known as magnetic variation.

navigation instruments Devices used to steer the course of a ship, plane, or other type of vehicle.

proportion The size of a part of something in relation to the whole.

radar screen Radar is a device that locates objects using radio waves. This information is then displayed on a computer screen.

smugglers People who take goods into or out of a country secretly or illegally.

sulfur A light yellow powder that burns with a blue flame.

tidal wave A huge wave caused by land movement under the sea.

torpedoed Something that has been attacked or destroyed by a torpedo. A torpedo is a long, narrow explosive device that is powered by a motor and travels underwater. Usually fired from submarines at ships.

tracking signal The signal that appears on a radar screen to show the position of an object, such as an airplane or ship.

transparent Something that is clear, or can be seen through.

U–boat A German submarine. It is a term particularly used to describe German submarines from World War I and World War II.

wreckage The remains of a vehicle after a serious accident, such as a plane crash, shipwreck, or automobile accident.

Index

Further Reading

Abels, Harriett S. *Bermuda Triangle*, "Mystery of . . ." series. Silver Burdett
  Press, 1987
Barber, Nicola and Anita Ganeri. *The Search for Sunken Treasure*, "Treasure
  Hunters" series. Raintree Steck-Vaughn, 1998
Brenner, Barbara. *If You Were There in 1942*. Simon and Schuster
  Childrens, 1991
Gaffron, Norma. *The Bermuda Triangle: Opposing Viewpoints*, "Great
  Mystery" series. Greenhaven, 1995